silent gh as in light

Carey Molter

Consulting Editor Monica Marx, M.A./Reading Specialist

ABDO
Publishing Company

Published by SandCastle™, an imprint of ABDO Publishing Company, 4940 Viking Drive, Edina, Minnesota 55435.

Printed in the United States.

Credits
Edited by: Pam Price
Curriculum Coordinator: Nancy Tuminelly
Cover and Interior Design and Production: Mighty Media
Photo Credits: Comstock, Corbis Images, Corel, Eyewire Images, Hemera, Rubberball Productions, Stockbyte

Library of Congress Cataloging-in-Publication Data

Molter, Carey, 1973-
    Silent GH as in light / Carey Molter.
        p. cm. -- (Silent letters)
    Includes index.
    Summary: Easy-to-read sentences introduce words that contain a silent "GH," such as light, daughter, and highway.
    ISBN 1-59197-444-5
    1. English language--Consonants--Juvenile literature. [1. English language--Consonants.] I. Title.

PE1159.M654 2003
428.1--dc21

                                                                            2003048124

SandCastle™ books are created by a professional team of educators, reading specialists, and content developers around five essential components that include phonemic awareness, phonics, vocabulary, text comprehension, and fluency. All books are written, reviewed, and leveled for guided reading, early intervention reading, and Accelerated Reader® programs and designed for use in shared, guided, and independent reading and writing activities to support a balanced approach to literacy instruction.

Let Us Know

After reading the book, SandCastle would like you to tell us your stories about reading. What is your favorite page? Was there something hard that you needed help with? Share the ups and downs of learning to read. We want to hear from you! To get posted on the ABDO Publishing Company Web site, send us e-mail at:

sandcastle@abdopub.com

SandCastle Level: Beginning

Silent-gh Words

daughter

height

highway

light

night

thought

3

The light is red.

Bert thought he
knew the answer.

Ann's uncle measured her height.

Jan's daughter likes to float with her.

There are many cars and trucks on the highway.

The fireworks show was at night.

The Neighbor's Light

The neighbor's daughter
is naughty.

She often acts haughty.

She runs through the yard
at night.

She turns on the neighbor's bright light.

She does this
without much thought.

She always hopes
she will not get caught!

More Silent-gh Words

bough	sigh
bought	sight
dough	sleigh
doughnut	straight
drought	taught
eight	thorough
flight	though
high	weigh
knight	weight
plough	

Glossary

fireworks   a loud, colorful display of explosives set off on special occasions

float   to rest on the top of water

haughty   acting too proud and looking down on other people

highway   a main public road

naughty   to misbehave

About SandCastle™

A professional team of educators, reading specialists, and content developers created the SandCastle™ series to support young readers as they develop reading skills and strategies and increase their general knowledge. The SandCastle™ series has four levels that correspond to early literacy development in young children. The levels are provided to help teachers and parents select the appropriate books for young readers.

Emerging Readers
(no flags)

Beginning Readers
(1 flag)

Transitional Readers
(2 flags)

Fluent Readers
(3 flags)

These levels are meant only as a guide. All levels are subject to change.

ABDO
Publishing Company

To see a complete list of SandCastle™ books and other nonfiction titles from ABDO Publishing Company, visit www.abdopub.com or contact us at:

4940 Viking Drive, Edina, Minnesota 55435 • 1-800-800-1312 • fax: 1-952-831-1632